JONATHAN RAY

HOW TO BUY
WINE

JONATHAN RAY

HOW TO BUY
WINE

**ALL YOU NEED TO KNOW TO CHOOSE
THE RIGHT BOTTLE EVERY TIME**

RYLAND
PETERS
& SMALL

London New York

For Marina, with love

DESIGNERS
Leslie Harrington, Megan Smith & Paul Stradling
EDITOR Delphine Lawrance
PICTURE RESEARCHER Emily Westlake
PRODUCTION Gordana Simakovic
ART DIRECTOR Leslie Harrington
PUBLISHING DIRECTOR Alison Starling

First published in the UK & US in 2010
by Ryland Peters & Small
20–21 Jockey's Fields
London WC1R 4BW

519 Broadway, 5th Floor
New York NY 10012
www.rylandpeters.com

10 9 8 7 6 5 4 3 2 1

ISBN 978 1 84597 972 0

Library of Congress Cataloging-in-Publication Data

Ray, Jonathan.
  How to buy wine : all you need to know to choose the
right bottle every
time / Jonathan Ray.
    p. cm.
  Includes index.
  ISBN 978-1-84597-972-0
  1. Wine and wine making--Popular works. I. Title.
TP548.R2878 2010
641.2'2--dc22
                                      2009042149

Contents

Introduction

It's a great time to be a wine lover. Governments might be trying to tax it out of our reach and the health police might insist that it's bad for us, but despite their efforts, wine is more readily available now than ever before, in a wider range of styles from a wider range of countries. Oh, and whatever the puritans might say, enough tests and studies have been done to prove that when drunk in moderation wine is in fact good for us.

No country can boast a greater variety of wines on their shelves than the UK. It is the world's largest importer of wine in terms of money spent as well as the fastest-growing wine market in Europe. And not only are people drinking more wine, it's coming from further afield. Fifteen years ago, French, German, Italian and Spanish wine accounted for circa two-thirds of UK wine consumption. Today their market share is down to one-third, as drinkers become more adventurous.

Things are changing in the US too; the country is set to become the world's largest wine-consuming market by 2012.

When it comes to buying wine in a store or supermarket, knowing which bottle to pick can be a daunting task. So, where to start?

With this guide, that's where. If you keep it simple and learn the basics, you will become savvy enough to gain real pleasure from the wine you buy in no time at all.

With this guide at your fingertips, you will learn enough about grape varieties, wine styles and regions, not to mention food and wine matching, to make well-informed choices in supermarkets, wine merchants or restaurants.

I never laugh at those who say "I don't know anything about wine, but I know what I like." If you know what you like, then you are well on your way to knowing about wine. The trick is to find out what else tastes like it and where to get it. Don't be scared – come on in, the water's lovely!

Pronunciation Guide

Albariño Al-bar-inyo

Aligoté Al-ee-go-tay

Barbera Bah-bear-ah

Cabernet Franc Kab-er-nay Fronk

Cabernet Sauvignon Kab-er-nay So-vin-yon

Carignan Carry-nion

Carmenère Kar-men-air

Chardonnay Shard-er-nay

Chenin Blanc Shen-an Blonk

Cinsault San-so

Colombard Kol-um-bard

Gamay Gam-eh

Gewurztraminer Ge-vertz-tram-in-ah

Grenache Gren-ash

Grüner Veltliner Groo-ner Felt-leener

Malbec Mal-beck

Marsanne Mah-san

Merlot Mur-low

Mourvèdre More-ved-rah

Müller-Thurgau Moolah Ter-gow

Muscat Musk-at

Nebbiolo Neb-io-loh

Petit Verdot Petty Ver-doh

Pinot Blanc Peeno Blonk

Pinot Gris Peeno Gree

Pinot Noir Peeno Nwaw

Pinotage Peeno-taj

Riesling Rees-ling

Roussanne Roo-san

Sangiovese San-gio-vayzee

Sauvignon Blanc So-vin-yon Blonk

Sémillon Sem-ill-yon

Shiraz Shi-razz

Sylvaner Silv-arn-er

Syrah Si-rah

Tempranillo Tem-pran-eeyo

Trebbiano Treb-ee-arno

Viognier Vee-uh-nee-ay

Zinfandel Zin-fan-dell

Key Wine Words

Appellation (Fr) A geographical indication used to identify where the grapes for the wine were grown.

Blanc de Blancs (Blonk der Blonk) A white wine made from white grapes.

Botrytis [See Noble Rot].

Corked Term given to a wine spoiled by a diseased or faulty cork.

Côte (Fr) A vineyard-covered slope.

Crémant (Fr) French sparkling wines made by the 'méthode traditionelle' such as Crémant d'Alsace or de Bourgogne.

Cru Classé (Fr) Classified vineyard.

Cuvée (Fr) Special selection.

Demi-sec (Fr) The literal meaning is 'partly dry' but when referring to sparkling wines it means medium sweet.

Domaine (Fr) Property or estate.

Doux (Fr) Sweet.

Frizzante (It) Sparkling.

Grand Cru (Fr) Top-quality wine.

Late Harvest A wine made from grapes picked late when they are at their ripest and sweetest.

Méthode Traditionelle The method by which champagne and all fine sparkling wines are made, with a secondary fermentation in bottle.

Mis(e) en Bouteille(s) au Château (Fr) Wine bottled at the property where it was made.

Moelleux (Fr) Sweet.

Mousseux (Fr) Sparkling.

Noble Rot The mould that makes grapes shrivel and rot, concentrating their sugars and making them ideal for sweet wine production.

Non-Vintage (NV) A wine blended from two or more different vintages.

Phylloxera A louse that attacks the roots of vines with disastrous results.

Pourriture Noble [See Noble Rot].

Rosso (It) Red.

Rouge (Fr) Red.

Sec (Fr) Dry.

Secco (It) Dry.

Seco (Sp) Dry.

Sekt (Ger) Sparkling wine.

Spumante (It) Sparkling.

Sur Lie (Fr) A wine that has lain on its lees. Lees are the yeasty residues that remains in the cask following fermentation.

Tannin The dry sensation in the mouth that is drawn from oak, pips and skins.

Terroir (Fr) The French term for everything such as soil, climate, exposure and that je ne sais quoi which influences a vineyard.

Varietal Wine made from a single grape variety.

Vieilles Vignes (Fr) Meaning 'old vines', these are thought to produce superior wine, due to their low yields and deep root network.

Vin de Pays (Fr) Country wine.

Vin de Table (Fr) Table wine.

Vin Doux Naturel (Fr) A fortified sweet wine.

Vin Ordinaire (Fr) Basic wine, not subject to any regulations.

Vino da Tavola (It) Table wine.

Vino de Mesa (Sp) Table wine.

Vintage The year of the actual grape harvest as well as the wine made from these grapes.

Storage

BASIC GUIDELINES FOR STORING WINE AT HOME

Any space that is dark, free from vibrations and strong odours and that has an even temperature (neither too hot nor too cold) can be transformed into your own personal 'wine cellar'.

Places to avoid include kitchens (except for everyday wine) and rooms near lift shafts and garages, since cooking smells and diesel oil are surprisingly pervasive and vibrations can shake up sediment. Studies, cloakrooms and the cupboard under the stairs are ideal, as is the space under the bed in the spare room.

SELF-STORAGE

If you want more than just a cardboard wine box on its side, invest in some wine racks. These can be bought ready made or custom built so as to fit the most unusual and awkward spaces in your home.

Temperature-controlled EuroCave wine cabinets are an excellent but expensive alternative if you have the money and the space. If price is no object, you can even have a steel tube containing a spiral cellar inserted into a hole dug into your drive or back garden.

TEMPERATURE

Wine likes to be cool, but isn't as fussy as people think. Between 10°C (50°F) and 15°C (59°F) is best, with 13°C (55°F) being the ideal. Much more important is maintaining a constant temperature and avoiding damp.

HOW TO STORE BOTTLES

Bottles should be laid on their sides to prevent the corks from drying out and shrinking. Fine wine in wooden cases should be left alone – the bottles will already be lying flat and, should you wish to sell them, unopened cases fetch a better price than opened ones.

IF YOU DON'T WANT TO OR CAN'T STORE WINE AT HOME

If you are investing in fine wine, then it is best either to store it with the merchant from whom you bought it or at independent, professionally run cellars. For a small annual fee (usually about £10 or $15 a year per dozen bottles), your wine will be kept in a perfect, temperature-controlled environment, making it easier to sell later on.

How To Read A Wine Label

In essence, wine labels are no different from the labels to be found on cans of baked beans or jars of coffee. They are there to give you all the information you need to make an informed decision about whether or not to buy the product. While front labels are strictly regulated, back labels often give a more detailed explanation of the wine. They might tell you which foods go well with the wine, what temperature it should be served at and so on.

OLD WORLD FRONT LABEL

The commune name or cuvée

The wine appellation

The vintage

The estate name

The type of wine

Bottled at the property where the wine was made

The producer's name and address

Country of origin

The wine's alcoholic strength and size of bottle

OLD WORLD BACK LABEL

The wine's description

Location of vineyard

Size of vineyard

Type of soil

Type of subsoil

Grape variety

Wine region

Health and allergy advice

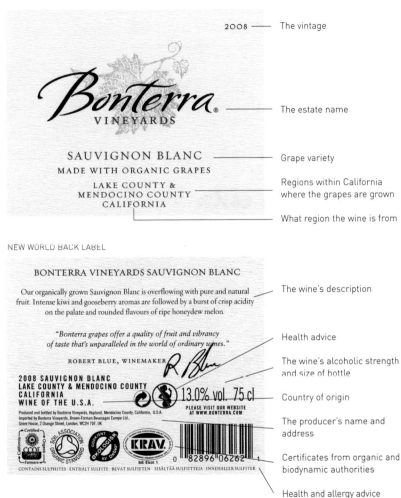

2008 —— The vintage

Bonterra ———— The estate name
VINEYARDS

SAUVIGNON BLANC ———— Grape variety
MADE WITH ORGANIC GRAPES

LAKE COUNTY & ——— Regions within California
MENDOCINO COUNTY where the grapes are grown
CALIFORNIA

——— What region the wine is from

NEW WORLD BACK LABEL

BONTERRA VINEYARDS SAUVIGNON BLANC

Our organically grown Sauvignon Blanc is overflowing with pure and natural ——— The wine's description
fruit. Intense kiwi and gooseberry aromas are followed by a burst of crisp acidity
on the palate and rounded flavours of ripe honeydew melon.

"Bonterra grapes offer a quality of fruit and vibrancy
of taste that's unparalleled in the world of ordinary wines." ——— Health advice

ROBERT BLUE, WINEMAKER
——— The wine's alcoholic strength
2008 SAUVIGNON BLANC and size of bottle
LAKE COUNTY & MENDOCINO COUNTY
CALIFORNIA 13.0% vol. 75 cl ——— Country of origin
WINE OF THE U.S.A. PLEASE VISIT OUR WEBSITE
AT WWW.BONTERRA.COM
Produced and bottled by Bonterra Vineyards, Hopland, Mendocino County, California, U.S.A. ——— The producer's name and
Imported by Bonterra Vineyards, Brown-Forman Beverages Europe Ltd., address
Grove House, 2 Orange Street, London, WC2H 7DF, UK

——— Certificates from organic and
CCOF SOIL ASSOCIATION EKOLOGISK KRAV biodynamic authorities
AV Odlat
SE Ekol 1 0 82896 06262 1

CONTAINS SULPHITES · ENTHÄLT SULFITE · BEVAT SULFIETEN · SISÄLTÄÄ SULFIITTEJA · INNEHÅLLER SULFITER ——— Health and allergy advice

◆ New World producers tend to market their wines by grape variety, while the Europeans don't (although this is changing), so it helps to know which varieties make which wines.

◆ Wines sold within the EU require the words 'contains sulphites' if they were made using sulphur and 99.9% of them are. Wines sold in the US require this too, along with a warning from the surgeon general as to the hazards of drinking alcohol.

◆ Neck labels are sometimes added to a bottle. These might state the vintage or a special feature of the wine, or display an award won.

Know Your Red Grapes

THE BIG FOUR

✦ **CABERNET SAUVIGNON** The big one, easy to grow, easy to drink and beloved of consumers and producers alike. Most famous for its role in the blended reds of Bordeaux, it flourishes almost everywhere that red grapes are grown, notably Australia, California, Tuscany and Chile. Typified by its blackcurrant aromas and flavours, and firm structure.

✦ **MERLOT** The major component of the wines of St Emilion and Pomerol in Bordeaux, it also makes superb examples in California, Chile and New Zealand. Although it is invariably blended with the firmer Cabernet Sauvignon in the Old World, it often stands alone in the New, being noted for its soft, supple fruit and silky elegance.

✦ **PINOT NOIR** The sole red grape of Burgundy and one of just three grape varieties permitted in the Champagne region. Despite being such a pain to grow (it's known as the 'Heartbreak Grape'), it is increasingly successful in Central Otago, Oregon, South Africa and Victoria. Noted for its juicy fruit when young and its vegetal and gamey notes when mature. Rarely blended outside Champagne.

✦ **SYRAH/SHIRAZ** Known as Syrah in Europe and Shiraz in Australia, it's big, full-flavoured and best known for producing Hermitage and Côte Rôtie in the Rhône Valley and rich, ripe blockbusters in the Barossa. Its wines are deep, dark and concentrated with hints of damsons, plums, pepper and spice. Often softened with a dash of white Viognier.

THE OTHER PLAYERS

✦ **BARBERA** Mainly found in northern Italy (Barbera d'Alba &c). Its wine is high in acidity, low in tannins.

✦ **CABERNET FRANC** A staple of the Loire Valley in Chinon, Bourgeuil and Saumur-Champigny.

✦ **CARIGNAN** Makes dark, hefty wines in both Spain (as Cariñena) and Languedoc-Roussillon.

✦ **CARMENÈRE** Once celebrated in Bordeaux, now going great guns in Chile.

✦ **CINSAULT** Highly productive; used chiefly for blending in the Rhône and Languedoc-Roussillon regions.

✦ **GAMAY** The juicy grape of Beaujolais.

✦ **GRENACHE** Adds a fruity spice to Rioja (as Garnacha) and Châteauneuf-du-Pape blends.

✦ **MALBEC** Responsible for dark, violet-scented wines in France (Cahors) and Argentina.

✦ **MOURVÈDRE** Much used in southern France and Spain (where it's known as Monastrell) for hearty blends.

✦ **NEBBIOLO** The grape behind the intense, tannic wines of Barolo and Barbaresco.

✦ **PETIT VERDOT** Full-flavoured and dark, it adds backbone to Bordeaux blends.

✦ **PINOTAGE** Indigenous to South Africa. Juicy when good; 'burned rubber' when not.

✦ **SANGIOVESE** The main grape of Chianti. Velvety soft and full of bitter cherry flavours.

✦ **TEMPRANILLO** Found throughout Spain, it's the major grape of Rioja.

✦ **ZINFANDEL** California's own. Big, peppery, spicy and alcoholic.

Know Your White Grapes

◆ CHENIN BLANC A remarkably versatile grape, although much underrated. Most at home in the Loire Valley and in South Africa, it can make dry, medium or sweet wines, sparkling or still. At its best it is crisp and fresh, yet rounded and supple with elusive notes of honey.

◆ RIESLING Although its spiritual home is Germany, where it is used unblended to make elegant dry, medium and sweet wines, it is also grown increasingly successfully in parts of Australia with a cool climate, New Zealand and South Africa. Apart from Alsace, you won't find it in France. Associated aromas include petrol, apples and honey.

THE BIG FOUR

◆ CHARDONNAY The world's favourite grape, seemingly grown everywhere. Celebrated as the sole grape of white Burgundy and Chablis, it is also crucial in Champagne, used on its own or blended with Pinot Noir and Pinot Meunier. It has a great affinity with oak, and when aged in a barrel takes on full, buttery flavours, especially in Australia and California.

◆ SAUVIGNON BLANC Used unblended to make such fabled wines of the Loire Valley as Pouilly-Fumé and Sancerre. Also hugely successful in New Zealand, Chile, Australia and South Africa. In Bordeaux it is often blended with Sémillon to make the great sweet wines of Sauternes. Easily identified thanks to its aromas of cut grass, herbs, asparagus and, yep, cat's pee.

THE OTHER PLAYERS

✦ **ALBARIÑO** Found in Spain and Portugal, making light, refreshing wines.

✦ **ALIGOTÉ** Rarely seen outside Burgundy where it makes unexciting dry wine.

✦ **COLOMBARD** Originally used for distillation, it also produces wines of crisp simplicity.

✦ **GEWURZTRAMINER** The spicy, peppery, lychee-like grape of Alsace.

✦ **GRÜNER VELTLINER** Austria's own, accounting for half the country's production.

✦ **MARSANNE** Mainly used in the Rhône in full-flavoured blends alongside Roussanne.

✦ **MÜLLER-THURGAU** A hybrid much used in Germany to make ghastly Liebfraumilch.

✦ **MUSCAT** Bizarrely, the one grape that makes wines that taste of, well, grapes.

✦ **PINOT BLANC** Widely used in Alsace and in Italy, where they call it Pinot Bianco.

✦ **PINOT GRIS** At home in Alsace, Germany and Italy (as Pinot Grigio).

✦ **ROUSSANNE** Often blended with Marsanne, it's permitted in both red and white Hermitage and Châteauneuf-du-Pape.

✦ **SÉMILLON** Popular in Australia for dry single varietals and in Bordeaux as part of dry or sweet blends.

✦ **SYLVANER** A pleasant but unexciting grape found in Alsace, Austria, Germany and Switzerland.

✦ **TREBBIANO** Also known as Ugni Blanc. Used for distillation or for bland white wines.

✦ **VIOGNIER** Madly fashionable at the moment, making seductive wines redolent of peaches and apricots.

France

France is the big one. Perhaps not in volume (Spain actually manages to produce more), but in stature. It's the wine-growing country against which all others are judged, its wines imitated and emulated the world over. To get a sense of the variety and sheer scale of what France has to offer, it's best to break the country down into its major regions.

ALSACE

Running along the French-German border, Alsace is one of the prettiest of all wine regions with some of the longest-established family producers, many dating back to the 1600s. In drinker-friendly fashion, the wines are labelled by grape variety and are predominantly white. Riesling is the big star here and is invariably much drier than the version from neighbouring Germany.

✦ **MAJOR GRAPES** Riesling, Gewurztraminer, Pinot Blanc, Pinot Gris, Sylvaner and Muscat for white; Pinot Noir for red.

✦ **TYPICAL STYLES** This is white wine country. In general, the wines are aromatic and spicy, ranging from crisp, dry, petrolly Rieslings to creamy, smoky Pinot Gris and sweet, luscious, lychee-like, late-picked Gewurztraminers.

✦ **KEY REGIONS** Alsace is comprised of one long stretch of vineyards tucked between the Vosges Mountains and the River Rhine.

✦ **GOOD FOR** Food-friendly wines.

✦ **NOT SO GOOD FOR** Reds. Pinot Noir is really only a bit player here.

✦ **WATCH OUT FOR** Crémant d'Alsace, a delightful sparkling alternative to Champagne.

BORDEAUX

Undoubtedly the most famous wine region of them all and home to the most structured and elegant of red wines known to the British as 'claret'. The big-name wines might be out of your price range, but there are great-value examples to be found in the so-called petits châteaux. Superb sweet wines are made too in Sauternes, Barsac and Ste Croix du Mont.

✦ **MAJOR GRAPES** Cabernet Sauvignon and Merlot for red plus Cabernet Franc, Petit Verdot and Malbec; Sauvignon Blanc and Sémillon for whites with a bit of Muscadelle for the sweet wines.

✦ **TYPICAL STYLES** Blending is key, with Cabernet Sauvignon-dominant blends on the left bank of the Garonne and Merlot on the right.

✦ **KEY REGIONS** Haut-Médoc, Pauillac, Margaux, St Julien, St Estèphe, Pessac-Léognan, Pomerol, St Emilion, Sauternes and Barsac. Look for great value satellite areas too, such as Lussac St Emilion, Lalande-de-Pomerol and Premières Côtes de Bordeaux.

✦ **GOOD FOR** Elegant, long-lived reds of great complexity and luscious, honeyed, sweet wines.

✦ **NOT SO GOOD FOR** Anything made from Chardonnay; it doesn't dare show its face here!

✦ **WATCH OUT FOR**
The increasingly tasty dry whites blended from Sauvignon Blanc and Sémillon, often overlooked in this primarily red wine region.

PRODUCER NAMES TO LOOK OUT FOR

ALSACE	Château Beau-Site
F.E. Trimbach	Château Cheval Blanc
Hugel	Château Cissac
Josmeyer	Château Fombrauge
Léon Beyer	Château Haut-Bailly
Rolly-Gassmann	Château Lafite
Schlumberger	Château Langoa-Barton
Zind-Humbrecht	Château Liversan
	Château de Malle
BORDEAUX	Château Margaux
Château d'Angludet	Château Rieussec

BURGUNDY

Burgundy is both one of the easiest yet also one of the hardest regions to get to grips with. Easy, because you only have to remember two grapes (Pinot Noir and Chardonnay); hard, because the wines are named after the villages in which they are made, the quality varying dramatically between the thousands of producers, domaines and négociants. The wines here are unblended. Familiar names include Nuits St Georges, Pommard, Beaune, Gevrey-Chambertin, Volnay, Pouilly-Fuissé, St Véran, Mâcon-Lugny, Rully, Puligny-Montrachet, Chassin-Montrachet, Givry, Mersault and St Aubin.

✦ **MAJOR GRAPES** Pinot Noir for red and Chardonnay for white.

✦ **TYPICAL STYLES** Steely whites such as Puligny-Montrachet or Chablis and rounded, buttery ones such as Meursault; earthy, vegetal, cherry-ripe reds.

✦ **KEY REGIONS** Côte d'Or (Côte de Nuits and Côte de Beaune), Côte Chalonnaise, the Mâconnais, Chablis, Beaujolais.

✦ **GOOD FOR** Chardonnays and Pinot Noirs made by winemakers with centuries of expertise.

✦ **NOT SO GOOD FOR** Value. Top-quality Burgundy ain't cheap.

✦ **WATCH OUT FOR** Revitalized, easy-drinking, Beaujolais and Bourgogne Rouge and Blanc.

Chablis
Auxerre

Dijon •
Côte de Nuits
Nuits St Georges •
Beaune •
Côte de Beaune

Côte Chalonnaise

The Mâconnais

Beaujolais
Rhône

Lyon •

PRODUCER NAMES TO LOOK OUT FOR

Antonin Rodet	Domaine Faiveley
Blason de Bourgogne	Joseph Drouhin
Bouchard Père et Fils	La Chablisienne
Domaine Armand Rousseau	Louis Jadot
	Louis Latour
Domaine Dubois	Simonnet-Febvre
Domaine Etienne Sauzet	William Fèvre

LOIRE

The Loire Valley, famed for its fairytale châteaux, runs for 1,000 kilometres from the heart of France, west to the Atlantic coast. Most of the wines here are white, the best-known of which include Sancerre, Pouilly Fumé, Muscadet, Vouvray and basic Sauvignon de Touraine. The reds, such as Bourgueil, Chinon and Sancerre (which can in fact be red, white or rosé) are light and refreshing. All are unblended as single varietals.

✦ **MAJOR GRAPES** Chenin Blanc, Sauvignon Blanc and Melon de Bourgogne (also known as Muscadet) for white; Cabernet Franc and Pinot Noir for red.

✦ **TYPICAL STYLES** Bone-dry, zesty, zingy whites from Sauvignon Blanc and Muscadet; rounded, honeyed from Chenin Blanc and light, quaffable rosés and reds from Pinot Noir and Cabernet Franc.

✦ **KEY REGIONS** Anjou-Saumur, Touraine.

✦ **GOOD FOR** Crisp, minerally whites that cry out for a plate of seafood or oysters.

✦ **NOT SO GOOD FOR** Big, full-flavoured reds. Forget it, there are none.

✦ **WATCH OUT FOR** The less well-known (and cheaper) Sauvignon de Touraine and examples from Quincy, Reuilly and Menetou-Salon.

PRODUCER NAMES TO LOOK OUT FOR

André Dezat	Langlois-Chateau
Domaine Filliatreau	Marc Brédif
Domaine Vacheron	De Ladoucette
Gratien & Meyer	Olga Raffault
Henry Pellé	Château de Tracy

RHONE

The Rhône Valley runs from Vienne in the north almost to Avignon in the south, and for viticultural purposes it is split into two. Most of the production is red, with many more wines being made in the south than the north, but fewer great ones. Names to conjure with include Hermitage, Côte Rôtie, Cornas, Saint-Joseph and Crozes-Hermitage in the north and Châteauneuf-du-Pape, Gigondas and Lirac in the south.

✦ **MAJOR GRAPES** For reds, Syrah in the north and Grenache in the south plus Mourvèdre, Carignan and Cinsault; for whites, Viognier, Marsanne and Roussanne.

✦ **TYPICAL STYLES** The reds tend to be big, butch and spicy, and the whites headily aromatic.

✦ **KEY REGIONS** The area is divided between the Northern Rhône and Southern Rhône.

✦ **GOOD FOR** Non-mass-produced, terroir-driven wines.

✦ **NOT SO GOOD FOR** Anything light, delicate and subtle.

✦ **WATCH OUT FOR** Satellite areas such as Vaucluse and Orange making copycat Côtes du Rhône at modest prices.

PRODUCER NAMES TO LOOK OUT FOR

Alain Graillot	Georges Vernay
August Clape	H. Bonneau
Delas Frères	J.L. Chave
Domaine de la Solitude	M. Chapoutier
Domaine du Joncier	Paul Jaboulet Aîné
Domaine Jasmin	Perrin et Fils
E. Guigal	Y. Chave

REST OF FRANCE

If you never bought another wine from France's most famous wine-growing regions but stuck instead to lesser-known areas, you would still die happy. There are crisp, undemanding white wines from Gascony in the south west; spicy, peppery reds from Languedoc-Roussillon in the south and delicate rosés from Provence. Familiar names include Minervois, Corbières, Fitou, Banyuls, Bergerac, Gaillac and Cahors.

✦ **MAJOR GRAPES** Mourvèdre, Syrah, Cinsault, Carignan, Grenache, Cabernet Sauvignon and Tannat for reds and rosés; Chardonnay, Viognier, Ugni Blanc, Colombard, Clairette, Marsanne, Roussanne, Gros and Petit Manseng for whites.

✦ **TYPICAL STYLES** Where to start? There's every style imaginable: red, white and rosé; sweet and dry; still or sparkling.

✦ **KEY REGIONS** Languedoc-Roussillon, Corsica, Provence, Bergerac, Jura, Savoie.

✦ **GOOD FOR** Variety. There's something for everyone.

✦ **NOT SO GOOD FOR** Pricey, iconic wines.

✦ **WATCH OUT FOR** Wines from top-class co-operatives.

PRODUCER NAMES TO LOOK OUT FOR

Domaine de l'Aigle	Domaine du Tariquet
Domaine Capion	Louis Latour Ardèche
Domaine de Trévallon	Producteurs Plaimont

Spain

With 68 official wine regions and more hectares under vine than any other country, there is much in Spain to tempt the wine lover: crisp, refreshing whites, soft, mellow reds, bargain-price Cava and the great, complex fortified wines of Jerez, Sanlúcar de Barrameda and Montilla.

The trouble is that quality can vary dramatically and it's tempting to look no further than Rioja, Spain's most famous export. Made from Tempranillo, sometimes with an additional dollop of Garnacha (as Grenache is known here), Graciano or Mazuelo, Rioja is divided into four different categories based on minimum ageing periods. After the most basic example (simply called Rioja), Crianza is the youngest, having spent at least a year in oak and a few months in bottle. Reserva wines are aged for a minimum of three years, with at least a year in oak, while Gran Reserva wines, the highest quality, spend at least two years in wood and three in bottle before being released.

Sparkling Cava, almost all of which is produced in Penedès, can be an absolute bargain, even though it is never as good as the Spanish seem to think. But with an annual production of 228 million bottles and exports of 139 million, why should they worry?

✦ **MAJOR GRAPES** Albariño, Parellada, Palomino, Pedro Ximénez, Verdejo, Viura, Sauvignon Blanc, Xarel-lo, Macabeo, Chardonnay for whites; Garnacha (aka Grenache), Mencia, Bobal, Tempranillo, Mazuelo, Cariñena, Cabernet Sauvignon, Graciano, Syrah, Monastrell (aka Mourvèdre) for red wines.

✦ **TYPICAL STYLES** A new, more fruit-driven style of Rioja is emerging, alongside its more familiar soft and oaky version.

◆ **KEY REGIONS** Rioja, Rías Baixas, Ribeiro, Rueda, Valdepeñas, Calatayud, Jerez, Bierzo, Somontano, Penedès, Ribera del Duero, Navarra, Toro, Jumilla, Priorat, La Mancha.

◆ **GOOD FOR** Sherry, Spain's gift to the world, ranging from bone-dry aperitifs to lusciously sweet digestifs.

◆ **NOT SO GOOD FOR** Sparkling wines as good in quality as Champagne.

◆ **WATCH OUT FOR** Soft, creamy Albariño whites from the north west of the country.

PRODUCER NAMES TO LOOK OUT FOR

Berberana	Marqués de Cáceres
Campo Viejo	Marqués de la
Chivite	Concordia
Codorníu	Marqués de Monistrol
Contino	Marqués de Riscal
CVNE (Compañía	Ochoa
Vinícola del Norte	Paternina
de España)	Torres
Durius	Vega de la Reina
Freixenet	Viña Albali

Italy

Some of the best wines in the world are Italian. Unfortunately, so are some of the worst. A sip of silky smooth Sassicaia can be heaven; a gulp of raw, acidic Pinot Grigio can be hell. It can be confusing too, with over 3000 different grape varieties for consumers to contend with, some of them deeply obscure. Even well-known wines such as Montepulciano d'Abruzzo and Vino Nobile di Montepulciano can be baffling – the one named after Montepulciano the grape, the other after Montepulciano the town.

Why take the risk with an unfamiliar Radici Fiano di Avellino, say, when you can play safe and knock back a more recognizable Australian Chardonnay? Because of the joy of discovery, that's why.

With so many different grape types grown in wildly diverse regions, from Alto Adige in the north to sun-baked Sicily in the south, there really is a wine for everyone; no other country can boast such variety.

Yes, Cabernet Sauvignon has reared its head – spectacularly so in Tuscany – but the real fun is in finding a wine unique to any given part of Italy that speaks of the land it is from and of the people who make it.

Not for nothing is Italy known as Enotria – the 'Land of Wine'.

✦ **MAJOR GRAPES** Arneis, Chardonnay, Cortese, Fiano, Malvasia, Moscato, Pecorino, Pinot Bianco, Pinot Grigio, Prosecco, Trebbiano, Verdicchio, Vermentino for whites; Barbera, Cabernet Sauvignon, Canaiolo, Corvina, Dolcetto, Merlot, Molinara, Nebbiolo, Nero d'Avola, Rondinella, Sangiovese (aka Brunello and Montepulciano), Pinot Nero for reds.

✦ **TYPICAL STYLES** Every style imaginable! From sparkling Prosecco and Asti, to crisp white Soave and Frascati, spicy red Chianti and big, blockbusting Barolo and Barbaresco.

◆ **KEY REGIONS** Abruzzo, Le Marche, Piedmont, Tuscany, Chianti, Alto Adige, Veneto, Trentino, Friuli-Venezia Giulia, Emilia-Romagna, Puglia, Campania, Lombardy, Liguria, Valle d'Aosta, Umbria.

◆ **GOOD FOR** Variety. You really will find something for everyone in Italy.

◆ **NOT SO GOOD FOR** Consistency.

◆ **WATCH OUT FOR** The sparkling wines of Franciacorta — worthy rivals of Champagne.

PRODUCER NAMES TO LOOK OUT FOR

Allegrini	Guerrieri Rizzardi
Alois Lageder	Inycon
Antinori	Le Terrazze
Boscaini	Malvira
Canaletto	Masi
Castello Banfi	Planeta
Donnafugata	Ruffino
Fontanafredda	Settesoli
Frescobaldi	Tedeschi

Germany

Germany is all about Riesling, a grape that shines here brighter than anywhere else, with the possible exception of Alsace and pockets of Australia such as the Clare and Eden Valleys. Oh, and unfortunately, Germany is also all about Liebfraumilch. To our eternal shame, the British drink more of this depressingly bland, semi-sweet nonsense than any other country. The Germans don't even drink it themselves, which must tell us something.

Every wine of note is made from Riesling, and the grape variety is almost always mentioned on the label. If the wine comes from the Rhine Valley, it will be in a brown bottle and a green bottle if it hails from the Mosel.

Other than the grape, producer name and vineyard, the important words to look out for on the label are the six levels of ripeness that determine the body and style of the wine. The lightest and quite often driest (usually off-dry) is Kabinett, followed by Spätlese and Auslese which can be both dry and sweet (look out for 'trocken' on the label, meaning dry). Then comes

Beerenauslese, Trockenbeerenauslese and Eiswein, all of which are intensely rich and sublimely sweet.

✦ **MAJOR GRAPES** Riesling, Müller-Thurgau (mainstay of the dreaded Liebfraumilch), Pinot Blanc (aka Weissburgunder), Pinot Gris, Sylvaner for white wine. Pinot Noir (known variously as Blauburgunder or Spätburgunder) for red wine.

✦ **TYPICAL STYLES** German Riesling comes in a wonderful variety of styles, from crisp and dry to fruity and off-dry and richly sweet.

✦ **KEY REGIONS** Ahr, Mittelrhein, Franken, Württemberg, Baden, Mosel-Saar-Ruwer, Nahe, Pfalz, Rheingau, Rheinhessen.

✦ GOOD FOR Good value, low alcohol wines to drink with or without food.

✦ NOT SO GOOD FOR Reds other than Pinot Noir; bone-dry whites.

✦ WATCH OUT FOR Increasingly attractive, new-wave whites made from Pinot Blanc; light, fruity, pale, almost rosé-like reds from Pinot Noir.

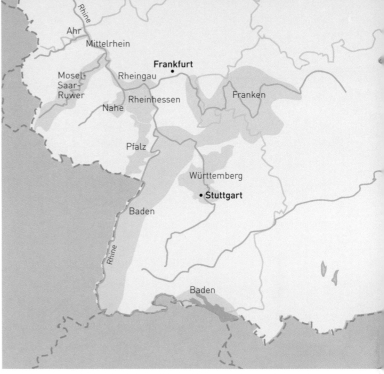

PRODUCER NAMES TO LOOK OUT FOR

August Kesseler	Josef Leitz
Baumann	Künstler
Carl Sittman	Louis Guntrum
Dr Bürklin-Wolf	Max Ferd Richter
Egon Müller	Reichsgraf von
Ernst Loosen	Kesselstatt
Fritz Haag	Robert Weil
Helmut Donnhoff	Schloss Johannisberg
JJ Prüm	Wolff Metternich

Portugal

Portugal is ideal for those who subscribe to the 'ABC' – Anything But Chardonnay/Cabernet – fraternity, as it has some fascinating wines made from local grape varieties you won't see anywhere else. Most exciting of all is the Douro Valley (the first wine region in the world to be officially demarcated in 1756), where port producers are now making some striking new-wave table wines.

✦ **MAJOR GRAPES** Verdelho, Alvarinho (also known as Albariño), Azal Branco, Rabiagato, Codega, Viozinho for whites; Touriga Nacional, Touriga Franca (also known as Francesa), Tinta Roriz (aka Tempranillo), Tinta Barroca, Tinta Cão, Baga for reds.

✦ **TYPICAL STYLES** Full-throttled reds from Dão and the Douro, and light, easy-drinking whites such as Vinho Verde.

✦ **KEY REGIONS** Bairrada, Douro Valley, Dão, Ribatejo, Alentejo, Algarve, Bucelas, Estremadura.

✦ **GOOD FOR** Fascinating, unique wines from unpronounceable grape varieties.

✦ **NOT SO GOOD FOR** Classic international grape varieties such as Cabernet Sauvignon or Chardonnay.

✦ **WATCH OUT FOR** New-wave reds from the Douro Valley.

PRODUCER NAMES TO LOOK OUT FOR

Lavradores de Feitoria	Quinta do Vale Meão
Niepoort	Quinta do Vallado
Quinta do Carmo	Quinta Vale Dona Maria
Quinta do Crasto	Real Companhia Velha
Quinta do Portal	Vida Nova

Other Regions

There's hardly a country that doesn't make wine these days. Don't just stick to France, but seek out something new for a change. If you don't like it, cook with it and avoid it next time. Here are half a dozen countries to keep your eye on.

AUSTRIA

Grüner Veltliner has rightly put Austria on the wine map. In the right hands it's one of the most delightful and food friendly of all wines.

CANADA

Some very decent reds and whites are made in British Columbia, but the Icewines of Ontario's Niagara Peninsula, from producers such as Inniskillin, Peller Estates and Jackson-Triggs, are truly among the wonders of the wine world.

ENGLAND AND WALES

Increasingly sophisticated, Champagne-rivalling, méthode traditionelle sparkling wines are being made by the likes of Chapel Down, Nyetimber and Ridgeview. Bacchus is proving a successful variety, producing some charmingly light and floral whites.

HUNGARY

Sweet Tokaji is one of the greatest of all vinous treats, but look too at the new-style dry whites made from Furmint.

LEBANON

Some excellent Bordeaux and Rhône-style reds are made here, the best-known of which are Château Musar, Château Ksara, Château Kefraya and Massaya.

SWITZERLAND

Swiss wines are rarely exported, which is a shame, as their reds from Pinot Noir and Gamay and whites, mainly from the grape variety Chasselas, are generally very enjoyable.

USA

Remarkably enough, every state in the Union now boasts a winery. And although California is streets ahead, not only in terms of quantity but also of quality, there is much to tempt the wine lover away from the region, most especially in Washington State, Oregon, New York and Virginia.

Mendocino
Sonoma
Napa Valley — Sierra Foothills
Los Carneros
Lodi
San Francisco — San Joaquin Valley
Monterey
San Luis Obispo
Santa Barbara
Los Angele

CALIFORNIA

Although California is notorious for mass-produced jug wine and the alcoholic sugar candy that is Blush or White Zinfandel (whereby red Zinfandel, responsible for some of the region's finest wines, is vinified as a white grape to produce a pale pink, overly sweet wine), it is also home to some of the most exquisite, elegant of wines, spoken of in the same breath as top Bordeaux or Burgundy.

Be it bulk or boutique, there is much to enjoy here such as the organic or biodynamic beauties of Mendocino, the classy blockbusters of Napa or the Pinots of Santa Barbara (you've seen Sideways, *right?).*

✦ **MAJOR GRAPES**
Chardonnay, Sauvignon Blanc, Viognier, Roussanne for whites; Zinfandel, Cabernet Sauvignon, Merlot, Pinot Noir, Barbera, Petite Sirah, Syrah, Sangiovese for reds.

✦ **TYPICAL STYLES** Spicy and intense red Zinfandels; smooth, concentrated Cabernets and Merlots; big, buttery Chardonnays; dire, semi-sweet Blush Zinfandel.

✦ **KEY REGIONS** Napa Valley, Mendocino, Sonoma, Santa Barbara, San Luis Obispo, Lodi, San Joaquin Valley, Monterey, Los Carneros, Sierra Foothills.

✦ **GOOD FOR** Big, dark Zinfandels and Cabernets of elegance and power as well as voluptuous Chardonnays.

◆ **NOT SO GOOD FOR** Chardonnays of subtlety and discretion.

◆ **WATCH OUT FOR** The wines of Mendocino, an agreeably wacky spot with a remarkably high proportion of organic and biodynamic wines.

PRODUCER NAMES TO LOOK OUT FOR

Andrew Quady	Iron Horse
Beringer	Jordan
Bonny Doon	Kendall-Jackson
Bonterra	Newton
Chateau Montelena	Opus One
Clos du Bois	Ravenswood
Clos du Val	Redwood Creek
DeLoach	Ridge
Duckhorn	Robert Mondavi
Fetzer	Sonoma-Cutrer
Firestone	Stag's Leap
Francis Ford Coppola	Suncé
Gallo	Trefethen

OREGON

Oregon is one of those rare spots where Pinot Noir is blissfully happy. Some superb, Burgundy-rivalling examples are being made in Willamette Valley, in some cases by Burgundians. The Pinot Gris and Rieslings aren't bad either.

And it's all happened so quickly. In 2008, 35,000 tons of grapes were harvested compared to 8,000 tons in 1998.

✦ **MAJOR GRAPES** Pinot Gris, Riesling, Chardonnay for whites; Pinot Noir, Merlot, Cabernet Sauvignon, Syrah, Tempranillo for reds.

✦ **TYPICAL STYLES** Pinot Noirs of ripe fruit and surprising subtlety; the same applies to the Chardonnays.

✦ **KEY REGIONS** Willamette Valley, Southern Oregon, Umpqua Valley, Rogue Valley, Columbia River Gorge, Walla Walla, Snake River Valley.

✦ **GOOD FOR** Pinot Noir. It just gets better.

✦ **NOT SO GOOD FOR** Big, blockbusting, Rhône-style wines.

✦ **WATCH OUT FOR** Up and coming Chardonnay; long dismissed here, it's beginning to shine.

WASHINGTON STATE

Washington State is the second largest wine-producing state in America, albeit a long way behind California. It boasts some 600 wineries, with production pretty much evenly split between red and white wine.

✦ **MAJOR GRAPES** Riesling, Semillon and Chardonnay for whites; Cabernet Sauvignon, Merlot and Syrah for reds.

✦ **TYPICAL STYLES** Crisp, dry, elegant whites and ripe, full-flavoured reds, reflecting the warm days and very cool nights.

✦ **KEY REGIONS** Columbia Valley, Yakima Valley, Walla Walla, Red Mountain, Puget Sound, Columbia River Gorge, Horse Heaven Hills, Wahluke Slope, Rattlesnake Hills, Snipes Mountain.

✦ **GOOD FOR** Vibrant, fruity reds; juicy whites.

✦ **NOT SO GOOD FOR** Sauvignon Blanc with much character.

✦ **WATCH OUT FOR** Rapidly improving Semillons, Rieslings and Syrahs.

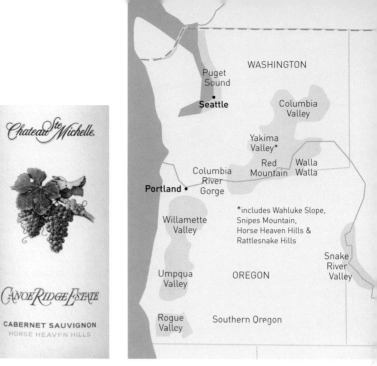

PRODUCER NAMES TO LOOK OUT FOR

OREGON	WASHINGTON STATE
Benton Lane	Cayuse
Cristom	Chateau Ste Michelle
Domaine Drouhin	Columbia Crest
Elk Cove	Duck Pond
Erath	L'Ecole No. 41
Eyrie	Hogue Cellars
Firesteed	Snoqualmie
Forest Grove	Washington Hills
Yamhill	Woodward Canyon

NEW YORK STATE

The third largest wine-producing state with vitis vinifera (classic European wine grapes), native and French hybrid varieties. Local varieties have a tendency to taste 'foxy', though, and are best avoided. The hybrids can be interesting and there are some fine sweet wines available.

✦ **MAJOR GRAPES** Chardonnay, Riesling, Seyval Blanc, Gewurztraminer, Vidal, Vignoles for whites; Cabernet Sauvignon, Cabernet Franc, Merlot, Pinot Noir, Baco Noir, Chambourcin, Concord for reds.

✦ **TYPICAL STYLES** 'Foxy' wines from native varieties; smooth Merlots and Pinot Noirs, Blancs or Gris; sweet, late-picked Vidal or Vignoles.

✦ **KEY REGIONS** Finger Lakes, Lake Erie, Cayuga Lake, Hudson River, Long Island, Seneca Lake.

✦ **GOOD FOR** Sound, if unexciting, Merlot.

✦ **NOT SO GOOD FOR** Native varieties; definitely an acquired taste.

✦ **WATCH OUT FOR** Tasty, late-picked dessert wines.

VIRGINIA

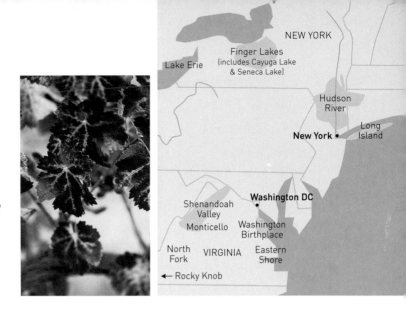

Knowledge of basic winemaking arrived here with the Jamestown colonists in 1607, with the first palatable Virginia wine probably being made from the appetizing-sounding Scuppernong grape.

Thomas Jefferson, fresh from ambassadorial duties in Paris, planted classic vitis vinifera varieties in 1789 and these are what the majority of Virginia's 140 plus wineries concentrate on.

✦ **MAJOR GRAPES** Chardonnay, Viognier, Vidal for whites; Norton, Tannat, Nebbiolo, Cabernet Sauvignon, Cabernet Franc, Merlot, Petit Verdot, Chambourcin for reds.

✦ **TYPICAL STYLES** Resolutely French in style, with a nod to Italy too.

✦ **KEY REGIONS** Shenandoah Valley, Monticello, Eastern Shore, Washington Birthplace, Rocky Knob, North Fork.

✦ **GOOD FOR** Stylish Bordeaux blends.

✦ **NOT SO GOOD FOR** Pinot Noir.

✦ **WATCH OUT FOR** Increasingly popular Viognier, all apricot and peach.

PRODUCER NAMES TO LOOK OUT FOR

NEW YORK STATE	VIRGINIA
Anthony Road	Barboursville
Bridgehampton	Kluge
Brotherhood	Leo Grande
Glenora	Mountain Cove
Lamoreaux Landing	Oasis
Wagner	Williamsburg

Chile

Chile is a bizarre shape: 2,600 miles long (roughly equivalent to San Francisco to New York or London to Dakar) and an average of only 80 miles wide. There are deserts in the north and ice fields in the south, mountains in the east and an ocean in the west. Such diverse geography inevitably means that the soils, altitudes and microclimates of Chile are remarkably varied and of great delight to pioneering winemakers. Added to which there are few vineyard pests and the dreaded phylloxera has never struck.

Chilean wines are approachable and exciting, and, in many cases, surprisingly complex. They are also extremely good value, which adds to their huge popularity. Indeed, for the first time ever, UK consumers are knocking back more Chilean wine than they are Spanish, thereby overtaking the US as Chile's biggest export market.

✦ **POPULAR GRAPES** Cabernet Sauvignon, Carmenère, Merlot, Pinot Noir and Syrah for reds; Chardonnay, Sauvignon Blanc and Viognier for whites.

✦ **KEY REGIONS**
Running from north to south are Elqui Valley, Casablanca Valley, Limarí Valley, Aconcagua Valley, San Antonio Valley (including Leyda), Maipo Valley, Colchagua Valley, Rapel Valley, Curicó Valley, Cachapoal Valley, Maule Valley, Bio Bio Valley and Malleco Valley.

✦ **TYPICAL STYLES** Spicy Syrahs, silky Pinot Noirs, chocolaty Carmenères, rich, dark Cabernet Sauvignons, zesty Sauvignon Blancs and buttery, rounded Chardonnays.

✦ **GOOD FOR VALUE** When Chile started to export, they came in cheap to grab a share of the market and have been slow to raise their

price points – lucky us! At both ends of the scale, the wines of Chile are invariably cheaper than those of equivalent quality elsewhere.

✦ **NOT SO GOOD FOR** Wines of Grand Cru status. Chilean icons such as Almaviva, Clos Apalta and Seña are almost there, but not quite. Watch this space.

✦ **WATCH OUT FOR** Crisp, aromatic Sauvignon Blancs that bridge the gap between the Loire Valley and New Zealand, increasingly sophisticated Pinot Noirs and deep, dark, intense Carmenères – a grape that was once popular in Bordeaux and that is now finding a whole new lease of life in Chile.

PRODUCER NAMES TO LOOK OUT FOR

Anakena	Matetic
Casa Lapostolle	Maycas de Limarí
Casa Marin	Miguel Torres
Casa Tamaya	Montes
Concha y Toro	Pérez Cruz
Cono Sur	Santa Rita
Cousiño-Macul	Tabalí
de Martino	Valdivieso
Emiliana	Ventisquero
Errázuriz	Veramonte
Haras de Pirque	Viña Carmen

Argentina

Argentina might seem like the new kid on the block, but in fact they've cultivated vines there for centuries and are currently the world's fifth largest wine producer. However, they have been slow to develop their export markets, largely because of the raging thirsts of the locals (who currently account for just under 80% of sales). But this is changing and more Argentine wines are being exported. And, thanks to massive local and foreign investment combined with low fixed costs and cheap land, their quality to price ratio is excellent.

Salta

La Rioja
San Juan
Mendoza
Buenos Aires

Patagonia

Argentina's vineyards are influenced by mountains and desert, their biggest advantage being altitude, meaning ripe, fruity wines with no loss of acidity. Growing grapes at an average of 900 m (3,000 ft) above sea level gives freshness, fruit and complexity.

The vast majority of wines come from Mendoza, and although some tasty Cabernets and Merlots are made here, Malbec is indisputably the champ.

Once widely grown in Bordeaux, the grape is nowadays barely seen outside Cahors in south west France, and Mendoza is fast proving to be its spiritual home. Somewhere in style between Cabernet Sauvignon and Merlot, Argentine Malbec has colour, structure and wonderful fruit, ideal for making fine, competitive wines.

✦ **MAJOR GRAPES** Malbec and Bonarda for red and Torrontés for white are the most important, but classics such as Cabernet Sauvignon, Merlot, Syrah, Tempranillo, Chardonnay, Pinot Gris and Viognier are also grown.

✦ **TYPICAL STYLES** Violet-scented, ripe, soft, supple, fleshy, plummy, velvety smooth Malbecs, either unblended or with added dashes of Cabernet, Merlot or Syrah; charmingly aromatic whites from Torrontés.

✦ **KEY REGIONS** Mendoza, La Rioja, San Juan, Salta, Patagonia.

✦ **GOOD FOR** Intense, concentrated red wines for drinking alongside Argentina's national dish – steak.

✦ **NOT SO GOOD FOR** Anything light and delicate in flavour.

✦ **WATCH OUT FOR** Torrontés, a deliciously spicy, floral (and modestly-priced) alternative to Chardonnay or Sauvignon Blanc.

PRODUCER NAMES TO LOOK OUT FOR

Caro	Finca Sophenia
Catena Zapata	Jean Bousquet
Cheval des Andes	La Riojana
Clos de los Siete	O. Fournier
Dominio del Plata	Salentein
F&J Lurton	Santa Celina
Familia Zuccardi	San Telmo
Finca Flichman	Trapiche
Finca Las Moras	Viñalba

Australia

Today, Australia is the leader in many of its markets; something that has happened comparatively quickly. After all, it wasn't that long ago that we were chortling at the sole Aussie offerings in the off-licence: Kanga Rouge and Wallaby White. How times have changed. Today in the UK, Australia's most important and lucrative market, one in every five bottles sold is Australian.

85% of these wines are from the big brands such as Jacob's Creek, Hardys, Banrock Station and Lindemans. They are safe, dependable, quaffable and great value, with lots of ripe fruit and easy-to-understand labels; in short, they are accessible. But the success of these brands has distorted consumers' views as to what is on offer if you spend a little bit more.

With 63 different registered Geographical Indications across the country (and 22 in Victoria alone) and over 2,000 wineries, there is much more regionality and terroir in Australian winemaking than most consumers realize, from big and bold Barossa to crisp and elegant Adelaide Hills, and we should not be afraid to splurge and trade up.

These big brands are proof that the country can produce excellent-value, accessible wines. But there is life beyond them, just as in France there is life beyond Piat d'Or. France is rightly celebrated for its diversity and it is high time that Australia was too. A whole new generation of regional wines is being produced in mature vineyards, planted with suitable varieties of grapes.

To take one example: Margaret River is some 2,625 miles (and three time zones) away from the Hunter Valley, which, to put it in context, is almost three times the distance from London to Florence. How's that for regional

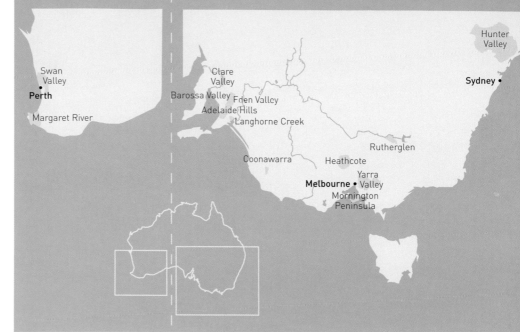

Hunter
Valley

Swan
Valley
Perth •

Margaret River

Clare
Valley
Barossa Valley
Eden Valley
Adelaide Hills
Langhorne Creek

Sydney •

Coonawarra

Heathcote

Rutherglen

Yarra
Melbourne • Valley
Mornington
Peninsula

variation? We don't go into a bar and ask for a glass of French wine, but for one of Bordeaux, Burgundy, Loire or Rhône. Why then do we ask for 'A nice Aussie white' instead of one from Margaret River, Clare Valley, Mornington Peninsula or Tasmania?

We can partly blame the Australians themselves for our ignorance. The large wine companies' practice of making wine from blended fruit sourced from all over Australia has blurred the regional distinctions that other countries have been more careful to cling on to. The wines might be good value and

tasty, but they won't exhibit any regional characteristics. Hunt around, for there is much in this vast country to enjoy.

✦ **MAJOR GRAPES** Chardonnay, Semillon (spelt here without the 'é'), Sauvignon Blanc, Muscat Viognier and Riesling for whites; Cabernet Sauvignon, Merlot, Shiraz (aka Syrah) and Pinot Noir for reds.

SHAW AND SMITH

Pinot Noir
Adelaide Hills

✦ **TYPICAL STYLES** Chardonnay still rules as Australia's leading white wine but there are also crisp, bone-dry Rieslings, not to mention lovely sparkling wines, powerful Shirazes and Cabernets and wondrous, sweet Muscats.

✦ **KEY REGIONS** Margaret River, Clare Valley, Eden Valley, Coonawarra, Mornington Peninsula, Adelaide Hills, Barossa Valley, Rutherglen, Heathcote, Yarra Valley, Hunter Valley, Langhorne Creek, Swan Valley.

✦ **GOOD FOR** Affordable, up-front, easy-drinking crowd-pleasers with easy-to-understand labels.

✦ **NOT SO GOOD FOR** Regional characteristics. Too many wines are still made from fruit drawn from right across this vast country, leading to unexciting uniformity and little hint of terroir.

✦ **WATCH OUT FOR** Cool-climate Pinot Noirs from Tasmania and Mornington Peninsula; crisp, zingy Rieslings from Clare and Eden Valleys; world-class sweet Muscats of Rutherglen, northern Victoria.

PRODUCER NAMES TO LOOK OUT FOR

Andrew Peace	Mount Horrocks
d'Arenberg	Mount Langi Ghiran
Banrock Station	Nepenthe
Best's	Penfolds
Brown Bros	Peter Lehmann
Clover Hill	Rosemount
Coldstream Hills	St Hallett
Elderton	Seppelt
Geoff Merrill	Shaw + Smith
Glaetzer	Stonier
Grant Burge	Taltarni
Green Point	Tapanappa
Hardys	Tim Adams
Jacob's Creek	Tyrrell's
Katnook Estate	Yalumba
Knappstein	Yarra Yering
Leeuwin Estate	Wirra Wirra
Lindemans	Wolf Blass
McWilliam's	Vasse Felix

New Zealand

New Zealand remains a comparatively young wine-growing country and, with continual new plantings, the best sites for the best grapes are still being identified. The first ever New Zealand Sauvignon Blanc was produced as recently as 1974, not from Marlborough but from near Auckland. It was some time afterwards that the north of the South Island emerged as the obvious site for this variety, just as Martinborough and Central Otago have now laid claim to Pinot Noir.

And so it is that other varieties, the so-called aromatics such as Gewurztraminer, Pinot Gris and Riesling, are also now beginning to show their regional distinctions and class in this beautifully bewitching country.

Sauvignon's success has blinded many people to the potential of other varieties, and although it will always be top dog, in Marlborough at least, we will see more of the other varieties.

✦ **POPULAR GRAPES** Mainly Sauvignon Blanc and Chardonnay for whites, but increasing amounts of Pinot Gris, Riesling and Gewurztraminer; Pinot Noir, Merlot, Cabernet Sauvignon and Syrah for reds.

✦ **TYPICAL STYLES** Kiwi Sauvignon Blancs are inimitable; full of grass, herbs and tropical fruit flavours. Pinot Noir is fruit-forward and juicily accessible, while the Bordeaux blends of Hawkes Bay veer towards France in style.

✦ **KEY REGIONS** Hawkes Bay, Nelson, Gisborne, Central Otago, Marlborough, Martinborough, Auckland, Waiheke Island.

✦ **GOOD FOR** Great purity of fruit. New Zealand really is a clean, green land and this is reflected in the superb-quality fruit they get.

✦ **NOT SO GOOD FOR** Cheap wine. It's expensive to make wine in New Zealand, and although quality is high, consumers have to pay for it. Few knockdown bargains to be found.

✦ **WATCH OUT FOR** Aromatics. Everyone knows and loves the 'Savvy Blancs' of New Zealand and the ever-improving Pinot Noirs, but there are some stunning Rieslings — dry, off-dry and sweet — of great precision and beauty, as well as lovely, peachy Pinot Gris and voluptuously spicy Gewurztraminers. And the Bordeaux-style reds of Hawkes Bay have the French quaking in their boots.

PRODUCER NAMES TO LOOK OUT FOR

Alana Estate	Oyster Bay
Cable Bay	Quartz Reef
Cloudy Bay	Rippon
Craggy Range	Saint Clair
Forrest Estate	Seifried Estate
Foxes Island	Seresin
Millton Vineyard	Sileni Estate
Montana	Spy Valley
Mount Difficulty	Te Awa Farm
Mount Edward	Te Mata

South Africa

South Africa has come a long way. During its isolation, most of the country's wines were tired and dreary, with the reds often tasting of burned rubber and the whites of acid drops. But that was then and this is now. South Africa is currently the world's ninth largest wine producer with over 600 wineries and 6,000 wines and things have changed dramatically.

Chenin Blanc, best-known for its role in producing the great Vouvrays of the Loire Valley, and Pinotage have both improved in particular. Chenin has been grown in South Africa for over 300 years and is the most widely planted grape variety in the country at the moment, accounting for about 40% of the world's total crop. It used to be called Steen here and was a byword for thin, raw, acidic paint-stripper best used for distillation. Now it is treated properly and is producing the most seductive, honeyed wines.

A cross between Cinsault and Pinot Noir, Pinotage is regarded as South Africa's 'own' grape and has a notorious tendency to taste burned-rubbery, tannic and heavily baked. But it has been tamed of late and there are now some juicily ripe, elegant, fruity and silky examples to enjoy.

✦ **POPULAR GRAPES** All manner of grapes are grown, notably Cabernet Sauvignon, Merlot, Shiraz, Pinot Noir and Pinotage for reds; Chenin Blanc, Sauvignon Blanc, Chardonnay, Colombard, Riesling and Viognier for whites.

✦ **TYPICAL STYLES** Full-flavoured Bordeaux or Rhône-style reds; juicy, peppery Pinotages; rich Chardonnays, crisp Sauvignons and elegantly honeyed Chenin Blancs.

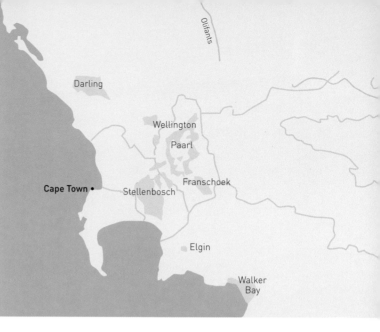

✦ KEY REGIONS Elgin, Darling, Stellenbosch, Franschhoek, Paarl, Wellington, Walker Bay.

✦ GOOD FOR Cheap and cheerful brands, affordable quality and one or two star wines.

✦ NOT SO GOOD FOR Low-alcohol wines. They tend to be big-boned beauties here rather than shrinking violets and it's not rare to find wines of 15% vol.

✦ WATCH OUT FOR New-wave Pinotage, where jam and spice have replaced burned rubber and tannin. And Chenin Blanc too, to rival the best that the Loire Valley has to offer.

PRODUCER NAMES TO LOOK OUT FOR

Ataraxia	Ken Forrester
Bellingham	Klein Constantia
Beyerskloof	Kumala
Boschendal	La Motte
Bouchard Finlayson	Newton Johnson
Elgin Vintners	Paul Cluver
First Cape	Raats
Flagstone	Rustenberg
Hamilton Russell	Spier
Iona	Sterhuis
Kanonkop	Vergelegen

Rosé Wines

Rosé is all the rage and worldwide sales are rocketing. But it's the classic chicken and egg question as to why. Are winemakers producing better rosé because consumers are demanding it, or are consumers demanding it because winemakers are producing better rosé?

Of course there is still vinous bubblegum such as Blush Zinfandel, Pinot Grigio and ersatz, pink Portuguese plonk made for the trading-up alcopoppers. But there is happily no shortage of 'grown-up' rosé too, made from the likes of Cabernet Sauvignon, Syrah and Pinot Noir.

At present, the sanctioned method of production involves pressing red grapes, leaving the resulting clear juice briefly on the skins (from where it gets its colour) before vinifying as a white wine. The only major wine region permitted simply to mix red wine (or juice) with white and stir is Champagne.

France is where many of us still head to find our rosés, and to Provence in particular, but there's hardly a country that doesn't make the stuff these days. California might still be the market leader in the UK, thanks largely to its aforementioned alcopops, but increasingly sophisticated examples are coming from Spain, Portugal, Chile, South Africa, New Zealand and Australia. Italy is also storming up the charts and not just because of its off-dry Pinot Grigio Blush. Pink sparkling wines abound too; (almost every major Champagne house has one) and there's even now an eyebrow-raising pink port on the market.

◆ **POPULAR GRAPES** Cabernet Franc, Cabernet Sauvignon, Gamay, Merlot, Pinot Noir, Pinotage and Syrah.

◆ **TYPICAL STYLES** They range from sugary, pink candy floss such as Blush Zinfandel, to classy, first-rate examples such as the best that Provence has to offer.

◆ **KEY REGIONS** Wherever grapes are grown these days, rosé is produced.

◆ **GOOD FOR** Drinking on their own or with all sorts of food where previously only a white or a red would have done.

◆ **NOT SO GOOD FOR** Partnering hearty roasts and stews.

◆ **WATCH OUT FOR** Pink sparkling wines. It doesn't have to be champagne; try a pink Prosecco or Cava.

PRODUCER NAMES TO LOOK OUT FOR

Château de Sours
Langlois-Chateau
Les Petites Jamelles
Louis Jadot
(all in France)
Tagus Creek (Portugal)

Chapel Down (UK)
Villa Maria (New Zealand)
Bonterra (USA)
The Real Rosé Company (various countries)

Sparkling Wines and Champagne

Champagne is the most celebrated (and most expensive) of all sparkling wines. It isn't the oldest though. That honour belongs to Blanquette de Limoux, a sparkling number made in the foothills of the French Pyrenees. Nor is champagne the most widely sold. Cava, which comes mainly from Penedès in Catalonia, Spain, far outstrips it, selling around 228 million bottles each year.

Fine Champagne, though, has a knack of making one feel good about oneself in a way that no other drink can – with the possible exception of a perfectly made dry martini. The term 'Champagne' guarantees only the wine's geographical origin, the method of production (secondary fermentation in bottle) and the grape varieties used (Chardonnay, Pinot Noir and Pinot Meunier) rather than its quality, and beware for there are some poorly made wines masquerading under the name. Look for other fine sparkling wines made by the same method from California, Australia, New Zealand and South Africa. Franciacorta in particular, from Italy, is a worthy rival.

That other famous Italian sparkling wine, Prosecco, is a joy, although it is made using different grapes and a different method. Be cautious of Cava, however. It might be the

most ubiquitous – and, invariably, the cheapest – of sparkling wines, but it can also give the biggest of headaches.

✦ POPULAR GRAPES Chardonnay, Pinot Noir and Pinot Meunier are the classic Champagne varieties, but Chenin Blanc, Riesling, Prosecco and Muscat also make fine sparkling wines. In Australia there is even a trend for red sparkling wine made from Shiraz.

✦ TYPICAL STYLES Champagnes and sparkling wines range from bone dry, crisp and zesty to rich, honeyed and sweet.

✦ KEY REGIONS Champagne; Penedès (mainly) in Spain for Cava; northern Italy for Prosecco and Franciacorta; Germany for Sekt. Added to which, all major New World regions produce decent sparkling wines these days. Heck, so does England.

✦ GOOD FOR Celebrations.

✦ NOT SO GOOD FOR Food, despite what the Champenois say.

✦ WATCH OUT FOR English sparkling wines made by the Champagne method (also known as the Méthode Traditionelle). Prosecco is also increasingly popular, and rightly so, being crisp, lively and relatively light in alcohol.

PRODUCER NAMES TO LOOK OUT FOR

CHAMPAGNE (FRANCE)	AUSTRALIA
Bollinger	Green Point
Louis Roederer	Jacob's Creek
Moët & Chandon	Wolf Blass
Mumm	
Nicolas Feuillatte	CALIFORNIA
Perrier Jouët	Mumm Cuvee Napa
Pol Roger	Roederer Estate Quartet
Veuve Clicquot	Schramsberg
CAVA (SPAIN)	ENGLAND
Codorníu	Chapel Down
Freixenet	Nyetimber
Marqués de Monistrol	Ridgeview
PROSECCO (ITALY)	NEW ZEALAND
Bisol	Lindauer
Trevisio L. e Figli	Montana
	Pelorus
FRANCIACORTA (ITALY)	
Bellavista	SOUTH AFRICA
Contadi Castaldi	Graham Beck
	Simonsig

Fortified Wines

Fortified wines are one of life's greatest treats and nothing to be scared of. Yes, they are higher in alcohol than other wines (typically being around 20% vol), having been 'fortified' with grape brandy before fermentation has ceased, but then you don't drink them like other wines. They are generally consumed either as an aperitif before a meal or as a digestif after one.

The most famous of fortified wines is port, made along the Douro River in northern Portugal and shipped to Porto (hence the name) and neighbouring Vila Nova de Gaia in order to mature, and sherry, made in Jerez and Manzanilla de Sanlúcar de Barrameda in south west Spain.

Other well-known examples include Madeira, from the Atlantic island of the same name, Marsala, from Sicily, and Muscat de Beaumes de Venise, from southern France. Fortifed Zinfandels from California and the Muscats of Rutherglen in Australia are well worth seeking out.

Port is divided into Vintage ports (from a single year, aged in bottle) that require decanting and Tawny ports (blends aged in barrel) that don't require decanting. Hybrid styles include Late Bottled Vintage and Vintage Character – cheaper but still delicious alternatives to full-blown Vintage.

Port has many rituals and traditions associated with it, the most obvious being the obligation to pass it to one's left at dinner. Some say this started in days of yore, allowing diners to keep their sword arm free in case of trouble. I think it's simpler than that: as any sailor will tell you, port is left and starboard right. Either way, there's no need to panic; such archaic traditions shouldn't get in the way of your enjoyment.

✦ **KEY REGIONS** The Douro Valley, Jerez, southern France, Madeira, Sicily, Victoria (Australia).

✦ **GOOD FOR** Aperitifs and digestifs; partnering pâtés and strong cheeses.

✦ **NOT SO GOOD FOR** Drinking throughout a meal – save it for the start or the end.

✦ **WATCH OUT FOR** Dry white port and Manzanilla sherry. Served well chilled, they both make invigorating kick starters to the appetite before a meal. Also, Croft's new pink port: not for the purists, but rather delicious.

✦ **POPULAR GRAPES** Touriga Nacional, Muscat, Malmsey, Sercial, Verdelho, Bual, Tinta Roriz, Moscatel, Palomino, Pedro Ximénez.

✦ **TYPICAL STYLES** Bone-dry Fino or Manzanilla sherries; rich, full-flavoured Vintage ports or nutty Tawny ports; lusciously sweet Muscats.

PRODUCER NAMES TO LOOK OUT FOR

PORTUGAL	MADEIRA
Cockburn's	Blandy
Croft	Henriques & Henriques
Dow's	
Fonseca	SPAIN
Graham's	Gonzalez Byass
Taylor's	Harvey's
Warre's	Lustau
	Barbadillo

Everyday Wines and Unsung Heroes

It's great to have a regular standby, but don't be scared to look beyond your favourite grape variety and region. If you slip up you can always use the wine for cooking with and at the very least, you will know better next time.

GOOD EVERYDAY WINES

✦ Italian Pinot Grigio and Soave make for good, regular quaffing, as do their red counterparts, Bardolino and Valpolicella.

✦ Languedoc-Roussillon just gets better, with wines such as Minervois, Corbières and Fitou improving with each vintage.

✦ Bordeaux isn't all about grand châteaux. There are some tasty blends on offer at the other end of the scale that make for great everyday drinking.

✦ There's more to California than the Napa Valley. Good-quality Chardonnays, Cabernets and Zinfandels abound in more reasonably priced Sonoma and Mendocino.

✦ In the UK consumers drink more wine from Australia than anywhere else. The market is dominated by the big brands, but look beyond these for characterful wines that speak of their particular regions. And, keep an eye on ever-improving South Africa.

SAFE BETS

✦ There are some wines that rarely let you down. Reliable Rioja produces soft, mellow, fruity reds to please most palates. Côtes du Rhône is usually good value for reds, while decent California Zinfandels are worth a look too. They should be full-flavoured and slightly spicy, and are great with hearty meat dishes.

✦ If you like your whites to be exuberant, try a New Zealand Sauvignon Blanc. It should be crisp and dry, but with plenty of exotic fruit flavours and zingy acidity, and as good on its own as it is with food.

✦ Some countries are good performers across the board. Chile, for example, produces excellent reds and whites that are, in general, absurdly underpriced.

UNSUNG HEROES

Wines that ought to be better known include the Sylvaners and Pinot Blancs from Alsace, which match food so well. Despite it being one of the oldest wine regions in the world, famous for its flamboyant Gewurztraminers, Alsace doesn't get the recognition it deserves for its other delicious wines.

✦ Austrian Grüner Veltliner, too, is still regarded as rather niche. Perhaps it's because the canny Austrians drink most of it themselves.

✦ Anything from Sicily. Still a bargain. And, don't forget how well most Italian wines go with food.

✦ English wine has now come of age and the top sparklers are fine enough to challenge the best that Champagne has to offer. Seek them out. You won't regret it.

✦ Look, too, for grapes that once flourished in France that now thrive in South America: Carmenère in Chile, for example, Malbec in Argentina and Tannat in Uruguay.

Party Wines

For large gatherings, keep it simple and don't offer too much choice. A red and a white should do it. If it's summer, why not just offer rosé? And don't forget the non-drinkers and drivers.

✦ Work on about half a bottle to a bottle per head. If in doubt, see if you can buy on a sale-or-return basis. Ask about quantity discounts when buying by the dozen.

✦ When chilling a large number of bottles, fill a bath or dustbin with some water and a little ice. To stop the labels peeling off, put the bottles in a bag before immersing them.

✦ Get ahead by pre-pouring the drinks.

GOOD STAND-ALONE WINES

✦ In general, wine is made to be drunk alongside food; together they often bring out the best in each other.

✦ That being said, there are some excellent wines that can be quaffed on their own. Pick a New Zealand Sauvignon Blanc; a bone-dry Muscadet; a succulent French Viognier; or an Alsace Pinot Blanc. Most rosés are great solo.

✦ Reds, too, can be delicious. Try a juicy Beaujolais; a Chilean Merlot; an Aussie Shiraz or one of the New World Pinot Noirs.

AFFORDABLE PARTY WINES

✦ Try before you buy, if you can; bargains aren't always what they seem.

✦ For bubbles on a budget, try Cava, Prosecco or any number of sparkling wines hailing from the New World.

✦ Red Côtes du Rhône or white Côtes de Gascogne make very decent party standbys.

✦ Chilean Sauvignon Blanc and Merlot are invariably good value and please most palates.

✦ For something a bit more quirky, try a spicy white Torrontés or a ripe and fruity red Bonarda from neighbouring Argentina.

Special-occasion Wines

Special occasions demand something fizzy. If money is no object, then go for vintage or prestige cuvée Champagne. Alternatively, set your sights a little lower and aim for non-vintage or supermarket own-label Champagne.

✦ If Champagne is *de trop* for the celebration you have in mind, try one of the many other fine sparkling wines that give northern France a run for its money. Italy has great examples such as Franciacorta and fine Prosecco. Top-quality Californian, Australian, New Zealand or even English fizzes are out there too.

✦ You can always jazz the fizz up and create simple cocktails by adding a splash of fresh fruit juice or smoothie, or by plopping a brandy-soaked sugar cube into each glass.

✦ At celebratory dinners, nothing looks more special than a red wine that has been decanted. It doesn't have to be a grand claret to be treated in such a way; even the humblest of wines benefits from being served in a decanter or carafe. And it looks like you've made an effort.

✦ If a special occasion starts with vintage Champagne, it should end with vintage port (which will need to be decanted) or a fine 20- or 40-year-old Tawny port (which won't). With port, you are meant always to pass the bottle or decanter to the left. But if the neighbour on your right is dying of thirst, I say ignore such nonsense.

✦ For romantic dinners à deux, keep some room for dessert wine. Nothing is more special or seductive than a post-prandial glass of well-chilled Sauternes, Muscat de Beaumes de Venise, Tokaji or Canadian Icewine.

Matching Wine to Food

Most foods go with most wines. In general the lighter the dish, the lighter the wine should be and the heavier the dish, the heavier the wine. Don't worry if you get it wrong; you'll know for next time.

SALADS AND LIGHT BITES

Antipasti Manzanilla or any crisp white

Barbecued ribs New World Shiraz

Blue cheeses Port

Caesar salad Smooth Chardonnay; Viognier

Ceviche New World Riesling

Charcuterie Cabernet Franc; Beaujolais; Côtes du Rhône

Foie gras Sauternes; Tokaji; German Beerenauslese; Canadian Icewine

Fritto misto Soave

Goat's cheese salad Sauvignon Blanc

Greek salad Retsina if you can cope; Grüner Veltliner if not

Insalata tricolore Pinot Grigio

Mushroom risotto White Rioja

Pesto Soave; Verdicchio

Pizza Chianti

Quesadilla Fruity Californian Pinot Noir

Quiche or onion tart Alsace Pinot Gris or Gewurztraminer; light Pinot Noir

Salade Niçoise Provençal rosé

Sushi and sashimi New World Chardonnay

Tapas Manzanilla

FISH AND SEAFOOD

Creamy fish dishes Rich, buttery New World Chardonnay

Dover sole Chablis or Macon

Dressed crab Viognier, especially Rhône

Fish pâté German Riesling

Fish pie New World Chardonnay

Goujons of sole Sauvignon Blanc, especially Sancerre or Pouilly-Fumé

Grilled king prawns New Zealand Sauvignon Blanc

Lobster Viognier; White Rhône

Oysters Chardonnay, especially Chablis

Pasta alla vongole (with clams) Pinot Grigio; Soave; Verdicchio

Salmon steak or Tuna Oregon or Central Otago Pinot Noir; Gamay

Salt and pepper squid South African Chenin Blanc

Scallops Grüner Veltliner

Seafood Muscadet

Seafood chowder New World Viognier

Seafood risotto Sauvignon Blanc; Sancerre; Pouilly-Fumé

Smoked salmon Champagne (dry)

Trout Alsace Riesling

Tuna carpaccio Chenin Blanc especially Vouvray

Turbot or seabass Classy Chardonnay (Burgundy)

MEAT AND POULTRY

Boeuf Bourguignon Red Burgundy or Zinfandel

Carbonara Australian Chardonnay

Cassoulet Cahors; Fitou

Chicken korma Viognier; Marsanne

Chilli con carne Argentine Malbec

Choucroute garni Alsace Riesling

Coq au vin Red Burgundy

Cottage pie Pinotage

Duck breast Red Rioja

Game Pinot Noir; Zinfandel; Valpolicella Amarone

Hamburgers New World Cabernet Sauvignon or Zinfandel

Lamb cutlets Barolo

Lamb kebabs New World Merlot

Lasagne Chianti

Meatballs Chianti or Valpolicella

Meatloaf Zinfandel

Moussaka Something Greek!

Poached chicken breast White Rioja

Pot roast beef Hermitage or Côtes du Rhône

Rib of beef Red Bordeaux or California Cabernet Sauvignon

Roast duck or chicken Cabernet Sauvignon blends

Roast lamb with rosemary Red Rioja

Roast pork Red Douro

Sausages and mash Red Beaujolais

Spaghetti Bolognese Bardolino, Valpolicella or Chianti

Steak California Zinfandel; Australian Shiraz

Tagine Moroccan or Lebanese red

Tandoori chicken Pinot Blanc; Beaujolais

Thai green or red chicken curry Australian Semillon; New Zealand Sauvignon Blanc

Tomato and basil pasta Pinot Grigio

Venison Grenache; Châteauneuf-du-Pape

SWEET THINGS

Cheesecake Muscat de Beaumes de Venise

Chocolate Tawny port; PX sherry; sweet Muscat

Creamy puddings Sauternes

Crème brûlée Sweet Sauternes; Monbazillac

Crème caramel Australian Muscat; Malmsey Madeira

Fruit puddings Sweet Muscat

Panna cotta Canadian Icewine

Pavlova Late-picked Riesling

Strawberries and cream Sweet Champagne

Tarte Tatin Tokaji

Vanilla ice cream Pedro Ximénez

Wedding cake Sweet Champagne

Matching Food to Wine

Wine is made to be drunk with food. Ideal pairings are easy to get right and hard to get wrong. It's a matter of individual taste of course but here are some tried and tested partnerships.

RED WINES

Beaujolais (See Gamay)

Bordeaux (See Cabernet Sauvignon)

Burgundy (Red – see Pinot Noir)

Cabernet Franc Charcuterie; simple cheeses

Cabernet Sauvignon (Bordeaux) Roast duck or chicken; rib of beef

Cabernet Sauvignon (New World) Juicy steak; hamburgers

Cahors Cassoulet; beef stew

Chianti (See Sangiovese)

Gamay (Beaujolais) Sausages and mash; salmon steak

Grenache (Châteauneuf-du-Pape) Venison or feathered game

Malbec Rare steaks; chilli con carne

Merlot (New World) Lamb kebabs

Pinot Noir (Burgundy) Boeuf Bourguignon; coq au vin; game

Pinot Noir (Central Otago or Oregon) Tuna steak or salmon

Pinotage Grilled lamb cutlets; cottage pie

Red Douro Roast pork

Rioja Rosemary roast lamb; saddle of rabbit; sautéed duck breast

Sangiovese (Chianti) Spaghetti Bolognese; meatballs; pizza

Shiraz (New World) Steaks; stews; barbecued ribs

Syrah (Hermitage/Côtes du Rhône) Pot roast beef; loin of pork

Zinfandel Steaks; meatloaf

WHITE WINES

Burgundy (White – see Chardonnay)

Chablis (Chardonnay) Oysters; grilled Dover sole

Chardonnay (Burgundy) Baked turbot or seabass

Chardonnay (New World) Sushi and sashimi; fish pie

Chenin Blanc (South Africa) Salt and pepper squid

Chenin Blanc (Vouvray)
Tuna carpaccio

Gewurztraminer Asian and fusion cuisine. Onion tart or quiche

Grüner Veltliner Scallops; creamy fish dishes

Pinot Grigio (Italy) Pasta alla vongole; insalata tricolore

Pinot Gris (Alsace) Quiche; onion tart

Pouilly-Fumé (see Sauvignon Blanc)

Riesling (Alsace) Choucroute garni; grilled trout

Riesling (Germany) Fish pâté

Riesling (New World) Aperitif; ceviche

Rioja Poached chicken breast; mushroom risotto

Sancerre (see Sauvignon Blanc)

Sauvignon Blanc (New Zealand) Grilled king prawns

Sauvignon Blanc (Sancerre/Pouilly-Fumé) Goujons of sole; seafood risotto

Soave Fritto misto; all seafood

Viognier (New World) Spicy chicken; seafood chowder

Viognier (White Rhône) Cold lobster; dressed crab

Vouvray (see Chenin Blanc)

White Rhône (see Viognier)

CHAMPAGNE

Champagne (dry) As an aperitif; smoked salmon

Champagne (sweet) Wedding cake; strawberries and cream

FORTIFIED WINES

Manzanilla Nuts; tapas

Muscat (Sweet) Fruit puddings; chocolate

Pedro Ximénez (PX) Vanilla ice cream

Port Blue cheeses

DESSERT WINES

Muscadet Seafood

Sauternes Foie gras; blue cheese; creamy puddings

Tokaji Tarte tatin; aged Gouda

Index

Where to Buy Wine

Supermarkets have better ranges than ever these days, thanks to their awesome buying power. But don't ignore the independents and online suppliers; they often stock wines from producers too niche or too small to be found elsewhere.

67 WINES & SPIRITS www.67wine.com

ACKER MERRALL & CONDIT www.ackerwines.com

ADNAMS www.adnams.co.uk

AMERICA'S WINE SHOP www.americaswineshop.com

AVERYS www.averys.com

BACCHUS www.bacchuswinestore.com

BERRY BROS & RUDD www.bbr.com

LAITHWAITES www.laithwaites.co.uk

MAJESTIC www.majestic.co.uk

ODDBINS www.oddbins.com

PRIME WINE www.primewines.com

SAINSBURYS www.sainsburys.co.uk

TANNERS www.tanners-wines.co.uk

TESCO www.tesco.com/wine

THE REAL ROSE COMPANY www.therealrosecompany.co.uk

VALVONA & CROLLA www.valvonacrolla.co.uk

WAITROSE www.waitrosewine.com

YAPP BROS www.yapp.co.uk

Picture Credits

Endpapers ph Alan Williams; page 1 ph Peter Cassidy; 2 image courtesy of Waitrose (www.waitrosewine.com); 4-5 ph William Lingwood; 6-7 ph Alan Williams; 8 ph William Lingwood; 9 ph Dan Duchars/wine cellar in a house in Surrey designed by Spiral Cellars Ltd (www.spiralcellars.co.uk/0845 241 2768); 10 courtesy of J.M. Chatelier; 11 courtesy of Bonterra Vineyards; 12-17 ph Alan Williams; 18 ph Alan Williams/William Fèvre, Grands Vins de Chablis, France; 19 ph Alan Williams; 20 ph Alan WIliams/Maison M. Chapoutier; 21l ph Peter Cassidy; 21r Photolibrary.com; 22-23 ph Alan Williams; 24l ph William Lingwood; 24-25 ph Alan Williams; 26l ph William Lingwood; 26r ph Alan Williams; 27 ph Francesca Yorke; 28 & 29a ph Alan Williams; 29b ph William Lingwood; 30 ph Alan Williams; 31l ph William Lingwood; 31r ph Alan Williams; 32l image courtesy of Cristom Vineyards, Oregon (www.cristomwines.com); 32ar ph Alan Williams; 32br image courtesy of Sokol Blosser Vineyards, Oregon (www.sokolblosser.com); 33 image courtesy of Chateau Ste Michelle, Washington State (www.ste-michelle.com);

34 both © Anthony Road Wine Company (www.anthonyroadwine.com); 35 both ph Alan Williams; 36 & 37r ph Alan Williams/Viña Errázuriz, Chile; 37l ph Alan Williams/Viña Concha y Toro, Casablanca Valley, Chile; 38, 39al&ar ph Alan Williams; 39b ph William Lingwood; 40-41 ph Alan Williams; 42al © Shaw and Smith (www.shawandsmith.com); 42bl ph Alan Williams; 42r image courtesy of Waitrose (www.waitrosewine.com); 43 both ph Alan Williams; 44 ph William Lingwood; 45al image courtesy of Waitrose (www.waitrosewine.com); 45ar © New Zealand Winegrowers (www.nzwine.com); 45b © Seifried Estate (www.seifried.co.nz); 46l ph Alan Williams; 46-47a © Erica Moodie; 48a ph Alan Williams; 48b & 49 ph Peter Cassidy; 50-52 ph Alan Williams; 53 ph Peter Cassidy; 54 & 55l ph Alan Williams; 55r ph William Lingwood; 56 ph Francesca Yorke; 57l ph Alan Williams; 57r ph Peter Cassidy; 58 ph Alan Williams; 59 ph Richard Jung; 60l ph Peter Cassidy; 60r ph Alan Williams; 61 ph Richard Jung; 63 ph Alan Williams.